STANLEY

the Claustrophobic miner

by Donny Abbott

illustrated by Bethie Tel

For my lovely wife Shawna and our little miners Jack, Owen, and Wyatt

Published by Black Rim Press LLC

Text copyright © Donny Abbott, 2020

Illustrations copyright © Bethie Tel, 2020

All rights reserved

ISBN 978-1-7359223-0-0

Printed in China

This is Stanley.

When he was a little boy he always liked playing in the dirt.

And so did his dad.

Stanley's dad was a miner,

and his dad was a miner,

and his dad was a miner, and...

...well you get the picture. Stanley wanted to be a miner too.

Every morning Stanley would
watch his dad go into the mine.

And every evening he would watch
his dad come out of the mine.

Stanley couldn't wait to grow up and go into the mine with him.

The thought of digging for gold and striking it rich was more than he could stand.

One day, Stanley's dad
woke him up and said,
"Let's go into the mine."

Stanley was actually going into
the mine with his dad.

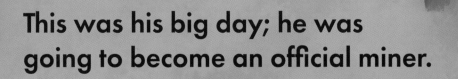

This was his big day; he was
going to become an official miner.

As Stanley traveled into the mine it became **darker** and **darker**.

The walls seemed to close in around him. His head started spinning.

He began gasping for air. He felt trapped. Stanley was **claustrophobic!**

To make himself feel better, Stanley began to sing a song:

*"I'm a claustrophobic miner,
a trapped forty-niner,
two hundred feet below..."*

How was he to know that he was **claustrophobic?**

It was a miner's worst nightmare.

What would his dad think?
What would his dad's dad think?
What would his dad's dad's dad think?

Stanley didn't know what to think.

He knew he had to think of something..... ....but what?

Suddenly he had an idea.

Stanley's mom always said that mirrors make rooms look larger.

Why not try something that would make the mine look larger, too? So that's what he did.

The next day, Stanley tied three mirrors to his waist and two to his boots.

Why, he even tied one to an elbow, an ankle, and also one tooth.

He strapped two to
each leg, one on the
front and one on
the back. And just
for good measure,
Stanley stuck one
straight out of his hat.

Then Stanley added more verses to his song, singing:

"I'm a claustrophobic miner,
a trapped forty-niner,
two hundred feet below.

"Wish I didn't have these fears,
that's why I wear all these mirrors,
to make the mine grow!"

And the mine did grow. He used his mirrors to make the mine look **larger.**

He felt a whole lot better...until he heard the other miners laughing at him.

"A claustrophobic miner,"
Scraggly scoffed.

And they all shouted,
"Look at those mirrors!"

"A trapped forty-niner,"
cried out Lefty.

Oh boy, Stanley's problems were getting worse. How could he turn this bad thing into something good?

He decided to turn the
mirrors on the miners who
were making fun of him.
That way they could get a
good look at themselves.

But it caused them to change.

And they all used Stanley's mirrors to look for gold in those hard-to-find places.

Scraggly got a haircut.

Lefty brushed his teeth.

It turns out that Stanley's mirrors did some good after all.

**Stanley smiled
and sang,**

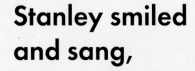

*"I'm a claustrophobic miner,
a trapped forty-niner,
two hundred feet below.*

*"Wish I didn't have these fears,
that's why I wear all these mirrors,
to make the mine grow!"*

The end.